Cover photo by Mario Todeschini
at Hurricanes Photographers Agency

Published by
Gardners

© Masterfoods 2006
® Whiskas is a register

ISBN 0-955354

D1340824

Purrems

A collection of cat poetry
by celebrity owners
and cat lovers

Thank you for buying The Whiskas® Book of Purrems.
We hope you enjoy this collection of cat poems, (or 'purrems')
and photography by celebrity cat-owners, journalists and
cat lovers up and down the country — from Jilly Cooper to
Fearne Cotton, Colin and Justin to John McCrirrick.

If you'd like to create your own 'purrem', we've left a blank
page at the back of this book. There's room to attach a picture
of your furry friend too!

At Whiskas® we love cats as much as you do, which is why
a contribution from every book sold will go to PDSA, the
veterinary charity that cares for pets in need of vets.
So while you're reading, you're helping to keep vulnerable
animals happy and healthy.

The Whiskas® Team

Our pets are at the heart of our lives and our pets' health and well-being is something that is of great importance to each and every one of us owners. Each year, PDSA provides an incredible 1.3 million free treatments to sick and injured pets belonging to people in need.

In many of those cases, the pet may be a person's only companion, or their one secure emotional anchor; so by treating a sick or injured animal, we help to make the owner feel much better too.

We have come a long way since PDSA first started providing free veterinary care in 1917. The first PDSA clinic was in a cellar in London's Whitechapel. Today, PDSA has 43 PetAid hospitals and four PetAid branches in towns and cities across the UK. Our vets and nurses treat broken legs, stitch cuts, help cure chronic illness and perform life-saving operations, all without charge. Our efforts mean that people who are less well off can still experience the pleasures and joys of pet ownership.

By purchasing this book, you have helped to ensure that the pets that come into our care lead the fittest, healthiest and happiest lives possible. Take pleasure from this delightful collection of 'purrems' and the joyful reminder they bring of what our cats mean to us.

Marilyn Rydström

Marilyn Rydström,
PDSA Director General

pdsa
for pets in need of vets

Every morning when I wake up,

And I see his little face,

I wonder how God

something so beautiful

Dog

could have created

Tracey Emin & Docket
Artist

ket!

S. W. A. L. K.

You came from a broken home,
A bit bewildered and alone,
Aged nearly three.
An Abyssinian tabby cross, with
Overwhelming love to give,

Alison Legh-Jones & Ben
Woman's Weekly Journalist

Especially to me.

J S Jevins with Clive & Oscar
Regional competition winner, West Yorkshire

We two are owned by our cats of whom we're proud,

One is quite shy whilst the other is quite loud,

One is Jet Black, the other is pure white,

And together we all sleep in OUR bed every night!!!

Pebbles the agoraphobic feline,
with eyes of brilliant green,

Your loving dad and a practising vet,
Yet you are far from lean.

Nervous and shy,
you sit on my knee,

A wonderful gift
that you afford only to me.

Scott Miller & Pebbles
Celebrity Vet

"You make me giggle every day.

You purr and prance away my tears.

You invade my bedroom at breakfast time, then wake me up by licking my ears."

Grace Dent – Missy
The Guardian Journalist

Mary Robertson – Tiddlywinks
Regional competition winner, North East

Along the catwalk
Models glide at measured,
practised pace,

While down the lawn
The true catwalk
Proceeds with nature's grace.

The cat's sleek body
Sways and gleams,
Her pawsteps dainty where,
So proud and queenly,
Tail curled high,
She takes the morning air.

Jilly Cooper & Feral
Author

I was a wild cat once

but my mistress tamed me

she called me Feral

no longer in peril

now i sleep by the fire

which is a change from the dark,

dark forest

My Whiskas comes in a tin now

And my milk in a cow

Vicky D'Ath & Purdey
Regional competition winner, East Midlands

My cat's name is Purdey

He is black with white paws

He loves the attention

But has very sharp claws

He has his own cat flap

He comes and he goes

But when he wants breakfast

Watch out for your toes!!

Sue Parslow & Ruskin
Your Cat Editor

We're friends me and my cat

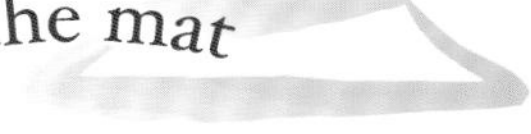

When I get home, he's there on the mat

He's beside me for breakfast

There again at tea

And when I go to bed

He's curled up waiting for me.

Alan Titchmarsh & Spud
TV Gardener

 is my cat
He is terribly fat
He got like that
From eating a rat
I fib, because he didn't really;
He got like that 'cause I love him dearly.
And when he asks for meat and biscuits in the morning,
I haven't the heart to issue him with
any kind of health warning
So I put tasty meat and crunchy biscuits
in both his stainless steel bowls,
And as a result, the young trees that are
trying to grow in my orchard are plagued with voles

He'd eat them if I gave him less biscuits and meat,
But he's just a cat I feel bound to treat
He's black with a white bib and four white paws,
And an appetite To rival Jaws.

John Scott – Norman & Nellie
This Morning Journalist

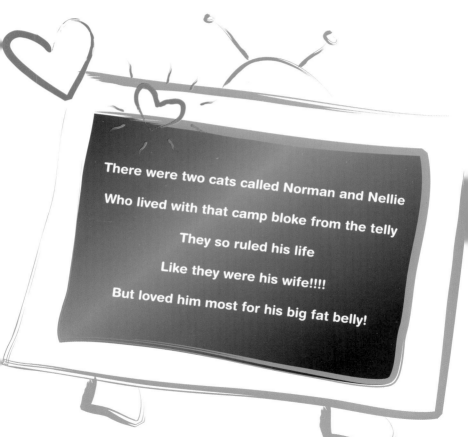

There were two cats called Norman and Nellie

Who lived with that camp bloke from the telly

They so ruled his life

Like they were his wife!!!!

But loved him most for his big fat belly!

Glenda Standing & Rafferty
Regional competition winner, Yorkshire

Why do I love you, why do I care?
I wake up each morning & if you're not there,
I'm out in my nightie, soaked in the rain,
calling out Rafferty over again,
You saunter towards me, your tail held up high,
my worry disperses, I've no need to cry,
you eat up your breakfast, then jump into bed.
and there you will stay, till next time you're fed

For Our Best Friend...

Colin & Justin with Their Best Friend
TV Presenters

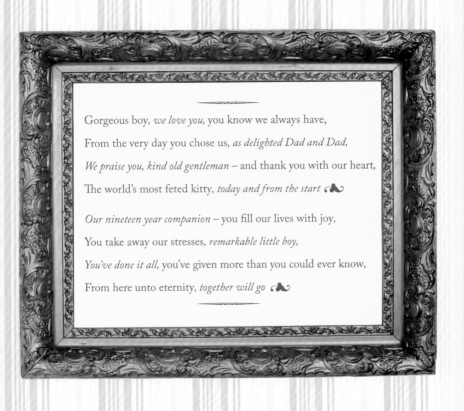

Gorgeous boy, *we love you*, you know we always have,

From the very day you chose us, *as delighted Dad and Dad*,

We praise you, kind old gentleman – and thank you with our heart,

The world's most feted kitty, *today and from the start*

Our nineteen year companion – you fill our lives with joy,

You take away our stresses, *remarkable little boy*,

You've done it all, you've given more than you could ever know,

From here unto eternity, *together will go*

When she was in Battersea
She was called Snowball
Which didn't make sense
Because she's black and white
So if she was a snowball
She'd have big bits of coal and grit in her fur
Now she's with me
She's called Chloe
And she's the friendliest, furriest, purriest cat
There's no grit in her at all
In fact, she's never even caught a mouse

Jane Common & Chloe
Take 5 Editor

TWO BEAUTIFUL CATS CALLED
BROWN AND BLUE

BROUGHT JOY AND DELIGHT TO MANY

BROWN LOVED HIS BED AND A LAP TOO

WHILE BLUE PREFERRED
OUTDOOR TERRITORY

NOW IN CAT HEAVEN BOTH UNITED

BUT STILL IN MY DREAMS
ARE OFTEN SIGHTED.

Caroline Corbould – Brown & Blue
Regional competition winner, East Anglia

Somehow I feel it's my duty to tell you about my top cat Lucy,

Liz McClarnon & Lucy

Singer

She is massively mental and wonderfully gentle

I love her so much she is a cutie

Heaven for me,
though some won't agree,
is Oscar by the bath
with his tail on my knee

Jenni Trent-Hughes, Writer and Broadcaster

Her Son, Jack, with Oscar

Oscar my cat, has
piercing blue eyes

He greets me in the
morning with a little surprise

A kiss on the cheek,
sets me up for the week

My "Caticus Raticus" treat!

Ashly Sloan-Brinkley and Oscar
Regional competition winner, London

Our lovely cats, Burlington and Bertie,

always rise at seven thirty

With a beautiful coat of cream and grey

when they're not curled up at the edge of my seat

they love to sleep and play

Summertime, sees them in the garden

which is their favourite place

we love to play hide and seek in the sun

where Burlington and Bertie hide without a trace

John McCrirrick with
Burlington & Bertie
TV Racing Pundit

Emma Lucas – Nelly
Daily Mail Weekend Journalist

Nelly is a curious cat
She is rather round and plump
She is the queen of the house and the neighbourhood
And can be a terrible grump

All day she sleeps on the spare room bed
Or on a newly washed pile of clothes
Only rising for a cuddle or to be fed
Or to wash her whiskers and toes

Her nose pressed against the glass tank
My pet minnows she tries to fish for
But with her teddy bear fur, and a very loud purr
A better cat I couldn't wish for

Samantha Bailey – Puss
Regional competition winner, North West

My cat likes to eat and
play with her toys
everyday she wakes up
to flirt with the boys
she struts around her castle
and purrs with all her might
but I know she'll be in my bed tonight

Daisy is an indoor cat,
she hates the wind and rain.
She prefers to press her little nose
against the window pane,
and when life gets too much for her
she takes to our warm bed,
that is, until, it is time for her
to come down and be fed.

Kim Woodburn & Daisy
TV Presenter

Matt Glass – Porky
The People Journalist

When I first set eyes on my kitten,
He was fighting his brothers for food
A bundle of fur with two massive ears
He was clumsy, noisy and rude.

But Porky's love for all kinds of grub
Didn't stop when I got him to mine
He just sits on the settee, watching TV
Waiting for next dinner time.

He doesn't catch mice or chase the birds,
Or do anything remotely 'catty'.
He chomps his way through anything tasty
And turns into more of a **fatty**.

But he likes to be stroked and lavished with praise
And his purr is a deafening sound
But he seems to forget when he lies on your lap
He's really **heavy**, and belongs on the ground.

Sophie Kemp & Sasha
Regional competition winner,
South East

Sleeping on the chair,
rolling in the sun,
our cat Sasha loves to have fun,
climbing the trees,
laying on the mat
that is why we love our cat.

Carley Stenson & Shadow
Actress, Hollyoaks

One day I met a very special cat.

I didn't know where she came from,

she just appeared on my doormat.

She came everyday,

and loved the biscuits I gave,

She would sit on my knee,

and my cuddles she would crave.

Anytime, anywhere around the

house I would go,

she would be right behind me,

so I named her my

shadow!

William Harston's
Schwarzenegger & Stallone
Daily Express Journalist

Hello, you've reached the answerphone

Of Schwarzenegger and Stallone

The ginger moggies living with Beachcomber.

But Sly is fast asleep,

While old Arnie's set to leap on a mouse

Well caught!

Give that cat a diploma!

A little black cat

Lost then found

Arrived at my door

Without a sound

Tired and weary he fell asleep

A special wee face I had to keep

Janet Thomson & Buttons
Regional competition winner, Scotland

Fearne Cotton & Keloy
TV Presenter

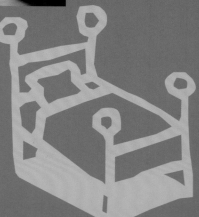

When it's time to snooze you're sprawled on my bed

When I wake in the morning you're curled around my head

When I walk down to breakfast you're under my feet

When I sit down for coffee you're pearched on my seat

When I'm typing on my laptop you walk on the keys

When I go to get up you jump on my knees

When I clean my teeth you sit on top of the loo

When I put on my socks you sit on my shoe

When I paint my face you nudge my lipstick

When I put on my watch you follow the hands tick

When I go to work you watch me go

 What you do when I'm out I'd love to know!!!

IF YOU'RE ALOOF WHILE HUMANS ALL ABOUT YOU
DISCOVER BROKEN PLATES AND BLAME IT ALL ON YOU,

IF YOU STAY CALM WHEN FURIOUS OWNERS DOUBT YOU
BECAUSE THEY KNOW IT'S YOU WHO STOLE THE STEW

IF YOU CAN SLEEP AND SLEEP THROUGHOUT THE DAYTIME
THEN WAKE AND PLAY THROUGHOUT THE NIGHT INSTEAD

THROUGHOUT THE DAY IGNORE REQUESTS FOR PLAYTIME
AND CHOOSE TO ROMP WHEN ALL HAVE GONE TO BED.

IF YOU CAN GO TO STUD AND KEEP YOUR VIRTUE,
THEN PROWL AT NIGHT TO FIND A COMMON TOM,

IF YOU'RE CONVINCED A VET WILL REALLY HURT YOU
AND DISAPPEAR AND SO REFUSE TO COME,

IF YOU REJECT THE SPECIAL FOOD THEY'VE BOUGHT YOU,
IF YOU SCRATCH LITTER WILDLY ROUND ABOUT THE FLAT

TURN UP WITH KITTENS WHEN THEY THINK THEY'VE SPAYED YOU
YOU ARE GRACEFUL, CHARMING, LOVELY – YOU'RE A CAT.

Celia Haddon & George
The Daily Telegraph Journalist

There was a young cat called Rosie

who loved to lick my toesies

she would sit on my lap

and have a good chat

then sleep all day in the roses

Nicola Wollacott – Rosie
Regional competition winner, South West

Busola Odulate – Charlie
Hot Stars Editor

We love our little Charlie
Although we nearly called him Malarkey

He is always up to mischief
And sometimes acts quite barmy

He hides in bags
And seems to laugh at our gags

He plays footie with a paper ball
With such speed he often runs into the wall

But he is as soppy as they come
And always has a kiss for mum

He loves being picked up by dad
Who is just potty over his "little lad"

He is far more fun than a night in a bar
Which is just why Charlie is such a star

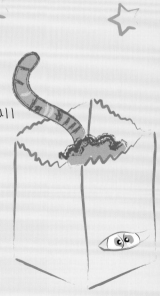

He crouches by the bluebells

Poised inside their screen

he doesn't twitch a whisker

and thinks he can't be seen

but just before he pounces

those wily birds take flight

the daft cat doesn't realise

his fur is brilliant white

Jean Penn – Jake
Regional competition winner, South

Sometimes quiet, sometimes fussy
beautiful Bengal, my name is Tussi.
Eyes like emeralds, burn like jade,
sparkle softly in the shade,
I stalk my toys, attack my mouse,
yes, I'm the tiger in our house.

Elly Boulton & Tussi
Regional competition winner, West Midlands

The 'purrfect' present

If you love cats, you'll love the Whiskas® 2007 calendar. It's packed full of pictures of cute cats and kittens. So it's an ideal present for all your cat-loving friends and family.

You can order your copy at www.whiskas.co.uk

Inspired?

The next two pages are yours to write your own purrem about your furry feline friend. You can draw, stick pictures, do whatever you want.

Have fun!

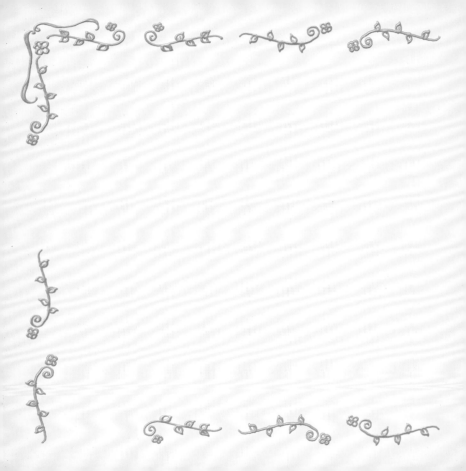

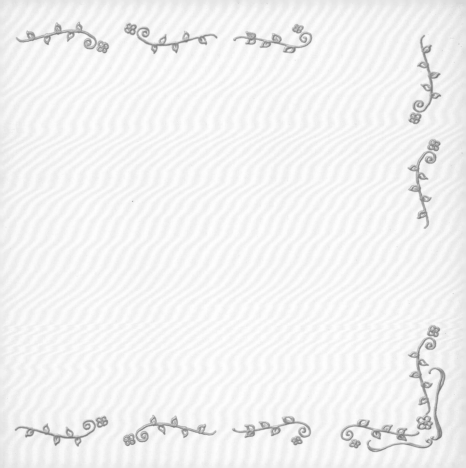